THE PORTAGE POETRY SERIES

SERIES TITLES

Red Camaro
Dwaine Rieves

The Coronation of the Ghost
Benjamin Gantcher

The Stone Tries to Understand the Hands
Susannah Sheffer

Where Babies Come From
Ori Fienberg

Cuttings
Hannah Dow

Forgive the Animal
Sarah Pape

Love as Invasive Species
Ellen Kombiyil

They Were Horrible Cooks
Allison Whittenberg

The New Life
Wendy Wisner

Restoring Prairie
Margaret Rozga

Table with Burning Candle
Julia Paul

A Bright Wound
Sarah A. Etlinger

The Velvet Book
Rae Gouirand

Listening to Mars
Sally Ashton

Glitter City
Bonnie Jill Emanuel

The Trouble with Being a Childless Only Child
Michelle Meyer

Happy Everything
Caitlin Cowan

Dear Lo
Brady Bove

Sadness of the Apex Predator
Dion O'Reilly

Do Not Feed the Animal
Hikari Miya

The Watching Sky
Judy Brackett Crowe

Let It Be Told in a Single Breath
Russell Thorburn

The Blue Divide
Linda Nemec Foster

Lake, River, Mountain
Mark B. Hamilton

Talking Diamonds
Linda Nemec Foster

Poetic People Power
Tara Bracco (ed.)

The Green Vault Heist
David Salner

There is a Corner of Someplace Else
Camden Michael Jones

Everything Waits
Jonathan Graham

We Are Reckless
Christy Prahl

Always a Body
Molly Fuller

Bowed As If Laden With Snow
Megan Wildhood

Silent Letter
Gail Hanlon

New Wilderness
Jenifer DeBellis

Fulgurite
Catherine Kyle

The Body Is Burden and Delight
Sharon White

Bone Country
Linda Nemec Foster

Not Just the Fire
R.B. Simon

Monarch
Heather Bourbeau

The Walk to Cefalù
Lynne Viti

The Found Object Imagines a Life: New and Selected Poems
Mary Catherine Harper

Naming the Ghost
Emily Hockaday

Mourning
Dokubo Melford Goodhead

Messengers of the Gods: New and Selected Poems
Kathryn Gahl

After the 8-Ball
Colleen Alles

Careful Cartography
Devon Bohm

Broken On the Wheel
Barbara Costas-Biggs

Sparks and Disperses
Cathleen Cohen

Holding My Selves Together: New and Selected Poems
Margaret Rozga

Lost and Found Departments
Heather Dubrow

Marginal Notes
Alfonso Brezmes

The Almost-Children
Cassondra Windwalker

Meditations of a Beast
Kristine Ong Muslim

"Picture yourself in a red Camaro, windows down in the sappy Mississippi air, radio on, Tammy Wynette's steel and twang, Daddy *yee-hawing* because 'red always wins.' Scenery streams by: boys and men together raw and naked through the trees, Daddy dressed for a casket, making passes at the nurses, 'the red cleft mud in sun-hardened / ditches, sweet gum and bramble…'—all that and so much more in Dwaine Rieves' astonishing new poem collection, *Red Camaro*. Hang on because, as we know, 'all we ever wanted was the ride.'"

—MARY-SHERMAN WILLIS
author of *Graffiti Calculus*

"These poems by Dwaine Rieves honor his Mississippi childhood yet reach out to the larger world as well, to confront the problem of evil. They honor 'the curious god within us' and are attentive to the healing power of the natural world. Layered, prismatic, and incisive, they explore both myth and faith to make 'every layer come together.' They bridge the gap between the life of the body and the life of the spirit with a resonant grace."

—GERALDINE CONNOLLY
author of *Aileron*

Red Camaro

poems

Dwaine Rieves

CORNERSTONE PRESS
UNIVERSITY OF WISCONSIN-STEVENS POINT

Cornerstone Press, Stevens Point, Wisconsin 54481

www.uwsp.edu/cornerstone

Printed in the United States of America by
Point Print and Design Studio, Stevens Point, Wisconsin

Library of Congress Control Number: 2024947478
ISBN: 978-1-960329-72-1

Cornerstone Press titles are produced in courses and internships offered by the
Department of English at the University of Wisconsin–Stevens Point.

DIRECTOR & PUBLISHER
Dr. Ross K. Tangedal

EXECUTIVE EDITORS
Jeff Snowbarger, Freesia McKee

EDITORIAL DIRECTOR
Ellie Atkinson

SENIOR EDITORS
Brett Hill, Grace Dahl

PRESS STAFF
Allison Lange, Sophie McPherson, Kylie Newton, Kaydee Rennie, Ava Willett

for Gregory Bolton

ALSO BY DWAINE RIEVES:

Shirtless Men Drink Free
When the Eye Forms

PRELUDE

The day of the storm I was flying home to visit family, to unwind and reconnect with the community. It was in Smithville that I first felt the urge to become a doctor, to maybe return some day and help take care of our people. In time I only came home to visit. And on that April visit, I arrived as the first rain started falling over destruction that reporters would soon call unimaginable. A tornado had leveled the town, the neighboring fields littered with family relics, a few survivors, and many bodies.

A day after the storm, Mississippi's Governor Haley Barbour joined a crowd of uniformed men mustering in the town's mangled heart. A reporter was tagging along and probably pleading for a statement, for the governor later appeared particularly defiant in his pictures. "We are hoping for the best but preparing for the worst." He said it after talking of the upcoming search for people on the list of the missing as well as those who may not have made the official list. He mentioned human remains. He closed with a kind of blessing, a recognition that we were all in this situation together. As if what happened here yesterday could have happened anywhere, which was important to remember because the dogs were already sniffing and strange men looking.

CONTENTS

Prelude   xv

Zeus   xix

STRANGE MEN

Factory, on Main   3

Abloom   4

The Boy   5

Just a Man   7

Power Take Off   8

Smart People   9

Vulcan   11

Initiation, in Blue and Eagle   12

Class Update   14

Crystal Bridges   16

One Theory   18

The Animal, Table 1   19

Tarzan   20

Jamboree   22

Vanilla   24

The Bull   25

COULD BE

You Should See the Moon Tonight   29

Men's Shop   31

Life Cycle   32

Tityus, In Black Chalk on Antique Paper   33

Overdrawn   34

Room Wallpapered with Conclusions   35

Nona   36

The Girl   37

Tropism   39

Pageant   40

Factory, One Town Over   41

When Asked What They Want to Do,
    Mavis Never Changes Her Answer   42

Stomach-down Before the World   43

The Animal, Table 2   44

In France, the Charolais Never Listen   45

Red Road   46

PLACES

Personalized Medicine   51

Last Ambulance Down Main   52

April   54

Initiation, in Because and Olives   55

Reflection   56

That Monday   57

Pearl Street Gardenia   58

Clarity   60

Six-Step Validation Elegy for Monroe Garment   61

Sediment   62

Ole Dog   63

Jack   64

In the Derelict Place, a Window   66

Heap   67

The Last Supper
    (With Men Under Controlled Conditions)   68

ICU 101: How to Intubate the Trachea   69

Blackberry Winter   70

Notes   73

Acknowledgments   77

Zeus

in the reflection
season, a mirror

pooled for the curious
god within us to float

upon and gaze over
as swans do in surface

delivery, creations
we've become astride

our utmost animal
as when knowing comes

like ripples stilled in
suspension, this essence

a swan might float
upon when alone

and uncontested, long
neck curved like a flaw

daring the great body
to bear it better

STRANGE MEN

"Meg: You're your own woman. Invite some people over.
Have some parties. Go out with strange men.

Lenny: I don't know any strange men."

—Beth Henley, *Crimes of the Heart*

Factory, on Main

There's a fresh sign before
        the empty building, local
numbers to call

if anyone's interested.
        Most kids left looking for a life
that came with money

to live it. Some stayed,
        saying money life takes might
otherwise take over

the living. There is a face
        to our system, options wrinkled, noses
flattened by nodding.

And always, phone
        lines open, folks waiting. Some pass
the factory daily, others

only when visiting where
        their folks started. Glass windows
are frosted, a selling point

if you don't want
        people on the highway to see
inside, as if they have

a choice, or that feeling
        of change on the cheek, something
breaking, and then the breeze.

Abloom

We had bought sheets that we perfumed with lavender.
But the smell never left.

—Patrick Modiano

We smell death in poked Styrofoam and sharp-
stemmed carnations. Comforting stuff

in a cologne's covering, thinning to turning
away, breath unlacing. We smell mist

splintering over a field's fresh-turned dirt, a father
pointing. We smell report cards and carbon

copies, Naugahyde stitched
into a purse, a mother looking for her wallet.

Death is reworking the sweet
stench of used equipment within our living.

We smell the taped-up odor of trying, the earthy
slug of outlived machinery, crinoline

on lay-away, the viewing hours. We smell
withering within muscles and pale, recoloring

facial stubble, companions
in parlors and cosmetics, air this world left us

working in raw in the clean cut
it tears through abloom, the wild mimosa.

The Boy

I

The boy grew up, became an electric
blender—great at whipping up

provocative daiquiris and unparalleled
smoothies. Surprised his parents.

Proud folks, each inconsolable
once he gunned his motor, the high button

taking him with it. In the visiting
hours, beside them we sat

on a sofa, tears on hands as they read
his journal out loud, of Jesus

and love where parents were
mentioned. Words, clear

as—no, no meaning ever follows
a blender's instruction manual.

As to questions, we keyed
louder, rehab humming, seasons

awhirl with recovery, a promising
birr, the unplugged grinding.

II

How can we fault our bodies when all
babies are born adorable?

We hold our breath, thinking
a breathless heart might keep

our children safer, hope full-
throttled. Jesus was too late to keep

Lazarus from dying. Probably dark,
tardiness prompting the unbelievable,

an overjoyed family, the reanimated
man from the sight of it all

stumbling. To blend in thereafter
couldn't have been easy, his story

mixed among others, separation
unbearable.

III

On this flight, there must be mothers
and far more fathers, a Bible in

a bag, someone hurting. Our night
is turbulent, fear high in the body. A jolt

makes a lady on the aisle close a paperback
in the light-pierced dark, as if she

can't bear the sight of words
in other people's stories, or even a haloing

of her body as she does what
she must within it, so she tightens

her seatbelt, hits the high button and
enters, by choice

unabashedly, the rumble of
the running engines.

Just a Man

Dogwoods bloom along roads
way back where Tammy Wynette was raised, her homeplace
not so far down the road from Tupelo.
       She made it out, big to
       boot, so men built a museum, walls
metal to concrete, anchoring rivets tornado-ready.
       You just never know. Still,

She would have liked it—our tour guide says—
this proud man speaking beside a churn of clipped
       dogwood, silk flourishing.
Jesus-blood, he suggests, the legend pink on a petal's
       dying tips. See, if blood could
       sing, every voice would
bleed out. But in here, Tammy's
       heart keeps pumping. Displays

suggest painted lips and promising
taffeta, a diploma from Tupelo Beauty College.
Dream big—but remember men
       sign the certificate.
       Headlines and headshots.
Disembodied gowns and hand-sewn sequins.
Just listen. "Stand by Your Man" rings

blood-pink in the exiting hall, a donation jar
glowing like our good guide, this man
       just a man along every road
       that takes you up to Tupelo.

Power Take Off

tough world this world
tough as farmers and tractors
with treacherous parts that turn
because it takes power in what
you hook up to a bush hog to
set the blades to turning
one for one with energy
transmitted via this semi-
phallic part that takes your
hands to hitch up to man-
ipulate until a spring-loaded
pin clicks into a place I often
thought I loved my mother
more than my father
thought love tougher
than a world I might work
out in if working might
click me into that place
where metal meets metal
in making me think love
might be farmed like a worry
of one or another my father
a fine but tough teacher
tougher than this tough
world is graspable by design
dangerous if you forget danger
powers the connection

Smart People

> Within the world
opposite ours, smart people were leaving
Baghdad, war plans prepared.

It will be better, I told my mother
though cancer staged four is, as smart
> people say, beyond good
> weapons.

> Beneath her clavicle
a port appeared, fluid in tubes, eyes turning
to a televised general fingering a vial
before smart people at the United Nations.

> Sub Q Neupogen didn't
help, red cells only hurt, and though
a tyrant could have done us in with what
smart people called weapons of mass
destruction, I kept telling her,
> *It will be better.*

> Iraqis buckled
under and though no battering
drug spared
a muscle, I insisted,
> *It will be better.*

Better, though it felt like a lie, my vial
of good intentions now empty years
later, a miracle missing.
> And yet, I'd trained

> with a doctor
who ordered saline injections
for demanding patients, the salty
sting relieving a pain beyond more
truthful therapies.

>> *It will be better.*
>> No questions asked.

> A decade and more
beyond, and the doctor in me needs
a shot, a morning when he quits awakening
in Baghdad, smart people saying

>> *it's only a visit.*

Vulcan

hero of forge and fire
        to forget or remember or
        maybe fear
much as to visit is to remember
        Birmingham, Alabama belongs
        to kinfolks decades back who had to
        go there we guessed to get
        better or beyond
a fear of troopers with big-city grins
        that tower much as
fear is an iron man five stories high
        people can point out to prove
fear is back talk from a god
        boned up in a hardening
        form once
fear is red poured
        hot from a massive pot
fear having been burnt into the body
        he's settling into with
fear most everyone can tell is running
        on fumes yes
it feels good to lie about fumes
        most every time they ask
        if we remember

Initiation, in Blue and Eagle

Classroom chairs moved out, windows
shaded—tonight, our Ag teacher's presiding
at his desk. Upfront, he's centered like Jesus

in the famous supper position, seniors
the apostles at his sides. Grins also, and
a banner—*Future Farmers of America*—

this membership we ninth graders
must now begin. Faces turn. Our teacher
smiles. *Welcome, men.*

Some stories are best plowed under, like seeds and surface
dirt—progress in action, whatever comes up unquestionably
natural. Even more so, if sprouts dither.

Mister Johnson couldn't be prouder.
He nods to our chapter president. So
to the largest closet, Andrew leads us.

To help with sprouting, seeds are best stripped from the hull,
production counted later. Another year the point, this time
deeper.

The deep voice says to undress, to wait
inside until a member calls us out.
The hull isn't us, so in silence we strip.

Fifty pounds of triple thirteen contains thirty-plus pounds of
filler. Run your hands through the granular and you'd never
know what's missing. That you'd never know is what some call
full recovery, nothing left but the mission, motto and creed.

The Last Supper for sure, this likeness
I repopulate later, for a disciple has called
the next new farmer to the door.

We welcome all newcomers, the pledge and jacket they take on, blue corduroy, thread gold in the emblem, a corn kernel perimeter, the cob like bread before an apostle, broken.

> The air is dank. It widens every chill
> to the door—Matthew and then another
> tenderfoot departing until, blindfolded
>
> and naked, I stand also before the cackling
> crowd. Small steps, they say, safe on the plank—
> two guys at my side, experienced hands
>
> holding as up the unseen ramp I walk
> and walk until our teacher says I must
> stop, let go, and—*Yes, Sir*—jump.

Farming takes risks and adult daring. Crops wash out, legs trip. By definition, faith is blindfolded, a licking inside your head, tongues maybe horses.

> Five feet up, maybe more. I have faith in
> our world and its teachers, losses where no
> bad part matters. A net below, maybe
>
> cotton. So, I do it. I jump and my luck
> lands manly loud, such hoot and hollering
> the cloth comes off, and I behold truth
>
> in my body unblinded, my fear such a silly
> thing, for the plank rests flush to the floor,
> two guys crouched at my knees, Thomas
>
> and John having slumped to make me
> believe. The master painted *The Last Supper*
> in plaster, its hiding room windows curiously

open. Behind the believers, mountains are blue, colors flaking—sky unstitched from earth, belonging from want, men from screaming.

Class Update

Fact is, Matthew
asked, so I helped look up a definition
of *felony*. Vivian quit

calling. Joanne wound up
selling greeting cards. A restocker, I'm told.
Walmarts in North Alabama.

Validated, they say.
Almost stable. Boatloads got by.
One tanked while scuba diving.

*Felony: from early English, a wickedness
or crime punishable by death
or mutilation.*

Disease redefined a number.
Creditors cashed in. Alice made money.
Matthew once said

initiation was good
as *family*, so no point in crying. Maybe
that's why he did what they wanted,

farmers of the future
laughing as Matthew sat naked, obedient
as a discharging toy. Some say

they're stuck, always in traffic.
Kids account for a lot. You might call it
a scuffle, years later, as one

teacher whispered, Matthew
acting out, something within him
triggered like a word

I have to believe
he was determined to outrun.
Caught on a curve, his

body was tossed
free, ringed by officers. Wheels
in the air. A total.

You can say Matthew paid
for a crime, though I have no idea what
the books cited.

He thanked me.
The ditch is wide, hard—thanks to
the sun, deep—

thanks to rainwater
and a world where no word helps when
the torrent runs.

Crystal Bridges

My cousin restocks Walmart
shelves, replacing empties with stuff made

for next to nothing *over the waters*, as folks once
called those places.

Discounts, my cousin says, help with the kids.

She's in it for life, my cousin
a people-person Sam Walton would be proud of,
as my family is, her hands in higher

gears once things leak or go bad, a ring
where the bottom stuck, a smear
where a bag gave.

              My cousin wipes away
the mess, so customers have no idea where
the stickiness ran, or why. I'm hoping

someday she might drive her kids up
to the hollow where Waltons charge
nothing to view

their fine, all-American art.
The museum arches over a creek where I stand
now musing and amused at rich

people connecting us to them across
"Crystal Bridges," a hokey name that could have been

              made *over the waters* for next
to nothing. But then it's my cousin

           speaking up
           from the water's sun-glint
           questions.

Another Walmart miracle, I suppose—
crystal fake but lapping on a surface
too busy for belittling, a process
                    my cousin's not about to wipe free

from an art made *over the waters*.
                    Yes. Walmart

places are a hard sparkle, she tells me.

Worth it though, once your water breaks
and pains come regular, hands
on steel in a bed

where you have to
push because you simply have to

once that gorgeous head starts crowning.

One Theory

One theory suggests evil exists because free will demands it, freedom

to hunt and hurt, choices hulking like animals above.

Fur brindled

to skin, I perch on a limb. Reach high to touch up my story, and

I turn. I imagine envy

the only evil angels are allowed to transport between this teasing

world and another answering *Maybe...*

I hear hounds

in eternal plunder, cries aloft skies no tree limbs can muffle.

My animal needs migrate

to every wild organ within me calling. Don't tell me

about yesterday.

There are yesterdays I lick to keep my animal parts from sticking.

The Animal, Table 1

Respond to allow a tally, including comments; where fur gave, the reasons

The animal wants	in suffering	No	It's pointless
to be alone:	in dying	Yes	The privacy in it, apart by choice
The animal craves discretion:	in concluding	No	It's pointless
	in healing	Yes	To crawl beneath the porch and watch
The animal wants to claw:	tomorrow	No	It's pointless
	today though, watching	Yes	Rain on the chinaberry bush, starlings in shiver
The animal wants a mother:	to see	No	It's pointless
	to cover	Yes	Heart like a wing, rubbing
The animal wants to forget:	its many wet tumbles	No	It's pointless
	the thuds though	Yes	Father watching, rain on a leaf, falling
The animal wants a distance:	from breath	No	It's pointless
	from knowing	Yes	Red in the rain, starlings the sound
The animal wants to change:	from the animal	No	It's pointless
	to the change	Yes	The animal found

Tarzan

I

Daylight revealed our bodies, our troop showering
wild among trees and improvised plumbing.

No scout laughed or pointed, but my feature felt
flawed from the beginning, my penis shrouded

like a loser in stark naked comparison. Weird
in its standout, wrinkled in a hoodie, fear clingy

as great vines our troop leader cut
with a machete. We redressed before grabbing

the vines, worshiped in covenant of high-leafed
muscadine and Tarzan imitation, every scout aligned

for takeoff and ape-man survival.

II

Legend says Mary preserved the holy prepuce
in oil, the concoction making its way

years later to another Mary, the sinful one
who had no idea why the oil smelled special, just

that it did. So when a famous Jew came
to visit, this second Mary anointed the Master

in a tincture of his own genitalia.

III

The other scouts push so every guy might swing
higher. Tarzan roars as soldiers make him

surrender. Mary falls to her knees before
the anointing. I smell all the skin I remember

not wanting, the odor of cut vines and sap
pearling, daylight raw within the liquid.

Jamboree

I

I pretended to sleep, my back turned before
tent-mates unzipped and started.

Can't help that. Can't help but smell
and remember. Rain hard, only canvas keeping

the storm beyond us. The boys whisper
behind my back, hands in secrets I feel

we share because good men share—
as the Master keeps telling us—troop

loyalty, let alone safety. An important
lesson, like learning knots. Takes discipline

and focus, right hand over left, a tip pulled
through the loop you have to leave open.

Time yourself, so your heart has more
competition. Evolving, the manual says.

God simply reworking his promise. Over
and over, the hymn a dirty angel sings, wet in his

Heaven. Master, how do we undo these ropes?
And night, why about us must it tighten?

II

My manual must be soaked, no pages free
to answer the grip behind my back, or explain

why rain contains so many sounds a post can't
make out loud until ropes come off.

III

The Master can't deviate from teachings just
as the disciples couldn't. But they did, I know.

Golgotha, the garden, probably rain. Facts not
unnatural the manual implies, Jesus no doubt little

different from Judas when it comes to the body.
I smell sweat that could have come from my father,

water dirt soaked up. Rain makes earth talk deeper.
Bowline and half-hitch, square knot and grannies

loop about an urge that demands to be followed
like an apostle. I know what the Bible says

about the body rolling over. We pitched our tents
beneath the trees. The manual said we shouldn't.

Leaves will do as they must after rain. I hear them
starting. Drop by drop, a wet knot slipping.

Vanilla

Why he preferred vanilla ice cream was beyond
me, simple as I suspected others would see us once
scooped out from our wishes, my father in overalls and me
admiring Neapolitan, vanilla still us but layered among
flavors far better than we were, strawberry supporting
our bland layer, chocolate up top like some God still
capable of grinning. I never knew why, my father's taste
maybe flawed without his knowing better. Maybe
we can live without knowing but I sure doubt anyone
can live without understanding. Light too bright
always tastes bitter. Vanilla ice cream drips like
every other version. A prism isn't a prism unless
it cuts light into many colors, but if you tilt another
crystal just right, every layer comes together.

The Bull

Between horizontal slats of unpainted fence—
2 x 6's rip-sawed to reveal tree rings, years stretched

lengthwise, dark on light, a universe
and more mapped out in natural stains—

there's a Charolais bull looking back, white-
coated and disturbed at being watched, head cocked

and ears distended, nostrils bulging
like the double darkness must in male species

when suddenly examined. I can't say I was
alone or lonely or before the old cow pen

by choice, or the bull perplexed by sawed-up years
framing me as a man trapped within

long slats of my own unearthing.
But when the nares flared, the god trapped within

me fixed all four feet on my myth
of self-transformation. The power was close,

Zeus in that eye so vocal, the bull blinked
when I called him *Father*.

COULD BE

"Nobody loves me but my mother, and she could be jivin' too."

—B.B. King

You Should See the Moon Tonight

I

You should see the moon tonight, hear
the cows talking. Usually, it's lunar

seas and craters, the view through
a hole in the barn's rooftop tin.

The near side leers like a lush
post-two martinis. I answered

because the cows were bawling.
Found an old girl's leg caught

within a gate, pinned in.
You should hear the freed

hussy quote Marvell.
Had we but world enough and time...

The great bull keeps snorting.
He can't believe what Marvell was missing.

II

You should see the moon tonight, hear
steers quoting critics, some calling

the harsh dishonest. Truth is,
I'm helping a troubled heifer

with calving. In calving, you reach
inside, grab the legs and pull.

You time your tug to contractions,
anticipating the big one.

III

The poets are squirming, and the bull
looks guilty.

IV

You should see the moon tonight, feel
the old drunk's gawking

as the new momma delivers. The calf
in a slimy beginning glistens,

the mother tonguing its coat, air clinking
in the bull's call for another round

of Marvell. Below the hole
in the roof, not a cow's lamenting time

or the moon you should see tonight.
The rowdiest has moved on to Millay

and once more the old bull's lusting.
The new calf stands, legs shaking

as it listens, the moon's voice low
and coy, our time enough, looming.

Men's Shop

My father wants a new suit, deep blue to black
for the viewing   loose fitting, with or without
a cuff

                                        A senior
discount, flat rate for cash money   All-weather
wool, just in case

                              As in the case
where the lid for my father's casket will be
                              open as he wants, so

people will see that he's prepared, no longer
on oxygen   So I call for a takeout

and take back if something's just not right
                              The best they have

As when people used to dress up for business
He's that kind of man now, formal

without my mother   She wanted
a closed casket, though I saw him look inside
                              when the director offered

and I saw how he saw
they had dressed her in the orange paisley
pantsuit she wanted   with shoulders

that give as when she was   working
the front desk of a business where every dressed-up
                    man had to stop

first to find out where to go
                              and who it was
he really needed to see

Life Cycle

the caterpillar stage of the catalpa sphinx moth
feeds on green catalpa tree leaves   in the human
being the formative stage of fulfilment feeds on green
feelings   I think   death I also think
is simply another stage of crawling

we sometimes feel time   I suspect
as a tree feels time   dirt and seasons simply
lived with like reasons   I could grow out of it
but for now   as I understand it catalpa trees evolved
to endure a moth's freaky beginning
I once saw them   caterpillars falling
from a catalpa tree as the luxurious leaves gave way
green eating green   all the way down

the tree limbs lay bare for they had borne
the process   it's a fact
not unlike the fact that the world is not mine
to change   or explain
noble to think otherwise   I thought until
I felt the telling crunch of leaves playing
dead beneath my feet   that sound
a change   a hope gnawing
on the limbs I hear high above this earth
          sap purling over
every place where the fluttering goes

Tityus, In Black Chalk on Antique Paper

In this drawing, the aging Michelangelo gifted the much younger artist Tommaso dei Cavalieri with a drawing prompt. The vulture pecking at the man's liver was a lesson imparting architectural knowledge.

Web Gallery of Art

Bed-bound and approaching eighty, my father made passes at his nurses.

The women were embarrassed to tell it, but did—reasoning as we did, reflex only, urge unearthed, an old man reaching…for relief?

For more devouring?

For some organ within him regenerating, some gift not for his body, but the ever-punishing beak above?

Not sin, grope not even danger.

My father would chuckle for no reason, cooperate with lifters. Magic dilates blackness, pain like eyes turning.

Sapphire, amazing.

The drawing is incriminating, my father taking more to be taken. Craving beyond the master, loss beastly about the art.

Red stiff as liver, the vulturine time at the lax belly keeps pecking. The artist himself slumped full frontal, hands arising, penis shriveled.

My father would smile, testicles round as ripe persimmons.

Overdrawn

My father never mentioned
Nixon, nor the *draft*, a cringe-worthy word

        for called-up or a chill, a banker's take
        on a payback plan. He never mentioned

a letter saying low is high, my draft number like lust
for a red Camaro, base price bare bottom in a 1970

        remake of the model. When I said they
        might keep it to remember, he said nothing

of black vinyl upholstery, bucket seats or an egg
crate grill, chrome lips befitting Nixon.

        Never thought he'd work
        out a draft on his account, a bank

statement in the mail, one column red monthly.
A stick shift no less, a chrome *C*

        on the hood, a *C* as in *Cambodia* or
        college, a fine ride though he never said

the draft had anything to do with those
six cylinders in a need I never guessed

        we shared. I doubt my father ever really
        feared Nixon, or years he knew

we could never outrun in a hot Camaro, a chill in every
red number where my rifle should go.

Room Wallpapered with Conclusions

We were proud for our time there

glad   regardless

graveyard shift   on-call

substitute or back-fill

time on a card   stamped

numbers shot black   that clock

stapling every twitch in our record

We work to understand the take-down

sound   We work to build

a place beyond it   home

these rooms we adorn in blue

or pink wallpaper   Here also

a choice in how we step over every

warp in the plank floors

Between the hours we work

and those we live out   O how

we work more to love than understand

a propane tank painted silver

Nona

Too far was never too much
with Nona at the wheel, plump arm propped
on a fin, her old car running like that senior year

we were graduating from, shoddy
but workable. Chauffeur diva, designated
driver when tomorrow might never otherwise happen,

our Nona would floorboard
the worry, Cadillac navigation her answer
to a distant god's calling. Years later I'll learn

a Roman deity was also
named Nona, Nona the mover and
shaker when it came to destiny—ancients convinced

Nona spun life along
timelines only the goddess knew.
No coincidence given our Nona, her sedan cruising

divine or parked solely
to pivot. At gathering thunder, canvas
arose like a coffin lid once Nona pushed a button, robotic

arms arising and rubber arching
above, our future impaled with a plop. Arrival
hugs have yet to undo the pink-faced drive into gamble.

Something indelible
about chance in a Caddy's wild ride, blown
shocks that set you flying into storms you know you

can't handle. Hold on—
the goddess shouts within me now, our Nona
winking as if she knows all we ever wanted was the ride.

The Girl

You speak like a green girl, unsifted in such perilous circumstance.
—Polonius, the father

I

the girl was pregnant

because she couldn't

bear it

rafters in the carport

in a fishing trailer a prince

hung herself

some say

white-washed

a rope to tie stuff down

might pull behind his pickup

II

some say once impregnated

hey non nony hey

the hooked one in

lure like love

the girl must bear it

how a fisherman lures

how connections also

before the king rises

III

the girl had a name

it could have started a sentence

the girl

from talk some say

the ropey connection

some say everyone knew

when speaking of

like a poem pulled

pray, you love

remember

IV

some say time heals

and the mold of form even

a memory

that makes the body remember

one choice within

hers with time

V

nameless is a need

as a girl hanging

say what it will

unbearable stuff

where the willow grows

by fear as by love

kind Lady, as unto us

the glass of fashion

as every moment bequeaths

a lure below the surface

its body is one

mine with me

like sweet bells jangled

visible from the street

her body, my Lord

nature of custom holds

we leave down

askance, my Lord

our bodies hold words

they say they're able

Tropism

jump they said and I jumped
I jumped and I would have jumped
had I known no bottom was there
there meaning I knew less
than belonging knows how
meaning means jump means order
means how wallowing takes you
to the sow's breast not knowing
where or how to jump but there
there they said look
see how it suckles there see
how it knows

Pageant

We are kids in a line, each with a gift to place below the manger.
We are stand-ins, symbols of needy
                  people in far-off places, how
                  they too must give what they can.
                  I'm dressed as a beggar

from Palestine, my box empty, the air inside it
from our place in Mississippi. My father
                  never made it out of Mississippi.
                  Just his army picture, dark hair wavy
                  as the night he almost slapped my mother.

God damn! No wife of mine smokes cigarettes! Like smoking's
against the law on wives in Mississippi.
                  My mother says he must think she shouldn't
                  work either. Wars play out like make-do
                  places in Mississippi—days her time

at the plant, four to midnight, his. A Salem or two before he gets home.
I use fly spray to clear the air before it's too late. Hides
                  the smoke. He'll never know. It works.
                  I think. He never says. Maybe
                  reminds him of places he didn't get out of

in Mississippi. Up close, the doll baby smells like plastic. Spotlights
shouldn't smoke but all stand-ins know better. Baby Jesus probably
                  cried more than he grinned, Joseph mired
                  in stink and Mary cussing, details my folks
                  don't talk about, this place that holy.

Factory, One Town Over

There is a face to our system

Paint wrinkling in words

Affixed to machines

That must be

Repaired with parts

Arriving from Memphis

Crates taking crowbars

To crack the blue

Line marked "open" in other

Places to make sure

We know how to handle

Precious components

In pine boxes big as

A small kid's casket

When Asked What They Want to Do, Mavis Never Changes Her Answer

What's your favorite color?
the preacher asks in children's church.
                    Red always wins.

And when you grow up, what do you want to be?
Mavis erupts, as always;
                    An artist!

But art, on average, pays far less
                    than programming, caregiving,
                    or gambling, these odds typical

enough to keep your hand on the hard
part of life's lever. See, it's tough to sit through
                    the service and not doctor
                    other people's answers, seeing
                    what I did with pressure.

Mavis is restless but drawing, sin naked
in the sermon, the preacher hepped up on a sin-prone
body, blue on yellow, orange recovering.

She's bound and determined to nub her crayons
to nothing, to gamble streaks the preacher
calls wasteful.
                    Let us rise now, fill the plate
                    with fear, worry, greed and all
                    the green apologies

Mavis keeps recoloring, purple wild beyond
the margins of our picture book bodies.

Stomach-down Before the World

He borrowed a cab-over camper insert, bolting
it to the bed of his little green pickup that summer

Atlanta skyscrapers stepped back from
streets, so country people could steer campers

with kids stretched out big-eyed body-to-body
in front-windowed nooks overhanging

the truck cabs, so when our teetering pickup
turned a corner my sisters and I gripped

a foam mattress that supported us stomach-down
before a world coming face-on with a speed

our daddy must have known would never exceed
what we could handle, top-heavy as we were

in hoping our daddy would never embarrass
his kids by tipping the whole contraption over.

What people might think was our main fear,
what we country people still fear when we pray

for daddies who take corners so fast kids must
learn more to feel than see, cars honking

and Georgia's Six Flags fluttering like God's
best welcoming banners, people camping

among what kids must hold on to, how
close we came, how high this world was.

The Animal, Table 2

Blacken the spot as urge would the animal:	☐ finding water, the animal thirsty
	☐ and, knowing better, slurps and tongues, one eyelid rising
	☐ to the hungry other, saliva like crystal, teeth for cutting
	☐ clear as a growl, which can't be water trickling
Imagine what the animal saw, then darken the spot most likely:	☐ an incident, a vicious Diana, goddess of hunters and chastity
	☐ appearing like anger, perplexed by urges—
	☐ to kill or unsex the animal, or growl with it
	☐ as a hunted male must, when threatened, turn throaty
If the urge has a future, then scale the animal's spot within it:	0 if the animal is threatened more by its growl than the goddess
	∞ if the animal can't help its thirst, or
	10 if, being male, the animal must mate or go dry in its tonguing
For the sake of respectability, state here the animal's satiety number:	
Then shade your personal thirst in the spot where you:	☐ swallow as the urge takes over, or
	☐ occur, like the lust in holiness, a yearning to
	☐ dwell, as she leers

In France, the Charolais Never Listen

Determined to outlive his body and two hundred
hungry Charolais heads, my father keeps wanting.

He wants to keep wanting as they do, craving
despite incredible bodies that come running

when he bangs a bucket. The cows never
get enough, so they rush the pasture's rusty fence

to ravish our neighbor's good hoe-garden corn.
Lust is typical for ivory-coated cattle bred to take

the southern French sun, which the want in
Mississippi outshines well beyond a spot

where barbed wire gives, so once
the head heifer pokes a hole and others follow

my father cuts out yelling like it's feeding
time. Foreign in sun-king fury, his wanting

voice makes the head heifer turn
her vivacious French eyes back to the broken

place where my father stands ready to
welcome the voracious animals, forever and again—

white coats aglow, proud tails swatting the flies.

Red Road

From asphalt to gravel, from gravel
    to bare earth—what I am
        searching for I do not know
    but I keep driving—this land
once home, years back
    my nature and teacher,
        my twang-mouthed preacher.
    Red cleft mud in sun-hardened
ditches, sweet gum and bramble
    wild below pines—this one lane
        only ruts in overgrowth
    drying. One bad turn and
my front axle's impaled on
    a stump, or windshield bashed
        in the oncoming rush of someone
    else leaving, another life
in clouding antic. Once I thought
    a way out was all I wanted, my goal
        less arrival than departure,
    relief merely going. Once
I dreamed of return in sapphires
    and feathers, triumphant chieftain.
        Once I gave up want's
    decoration, places where
someone's always talking
    of feathers. The gravel has quit
        and dirt's taken over. Tender
    me back, it says, too many
floor-boarders like you to
    remember, my lovers lost
        in new ways and old gullies.
    Maybe I'm wanting only
some overgrown ground

to update whatever within
          me I discarded, bad places
     maybe better now, the better less
angry. Maybe I'm wrong, this
     way all-natural in another
          time's uprooting. I want
     to know where the difference
between lost and loser
     must meet, this intersection
          where returning risks knowing
     head-on, the red road roaring.

PLACES

"One place understood helps us understand all places better."

—Eudora Welty

Personalized Medicine

A snapshot was all my mother recalled of her father.
Part-Choctaw she said. More josh
               than truth, I thought.
               More how to believe

than why believe. *Indian blood* she'd add, her
               good hand stirring
               a pan of ancestral opinions.

We ate as I hummed suspicions to the man's jarring
cheekbones and brow, a picture
that, after my mother died, prompted me
               to spit in a tube to confirm
               our Indian genetics.

Turned out, only the English and Irish showed up.

Imagination such bizarre medicine, my mother's
Choctaw father even stranger than results they said
to keep checking.
               Odd, but in time
               French and Germans appeared, Native
               Americans a possibility.

In time, my results quit questioning ingredients,
truth more Choctaw
               with every taste I remember.

Is truth simply the essence of good cooking?
Belief more nurturing than knowing?

Touch my face as my mother would touch it.
Now tell me—who's in the kitchen?

Last Ambulance Down Main

Daylight like an old bear
yawning, no siren sounding, no dogs
barking. And you

on the gurney, your eyes
closed as before us Main Street awakens
in amber, boarded up

storefronts hiding
ghosts only a dying mother can keep
working inside.

Bobby—the barber
pumping up little boys, one-by-one
to a clipping position.

Betty Sue—in postal
official trading stamps for pennies, time
red on every letter.

Dottie—the bank teller
counting dollar bills behind iron
bars, spittle on paper.

Miss Ora—pink in her
dress shop face going primrose
wild at the sight

of something perfect
for your youngest. I hold your hand
as we leave this

life forever, you
in a town that keeps Miss Ora
patting an infinity

of pressed cotton
pleats in a morning when I can't
help but think

you are already
telling her not to worry because—
over a distance

no one
ever wanted to outlive—it still
looks darling.

April

April is something to believe in
A tender sunlight trying again
A fleeting thing, here then not
You as you were, and are, a lot
To believe in when whatever
We were April never forgot

Initiation, in Because and Olives

...You don't love because: you love despite; not for the virtues but despite the faults.
—William Faulkner

Because to farm is to garden is to game
       is to laugh is to lose and also eat
because we must the leftovers

Because butt-nakedness and olives belong
       they said up where every new guy must
race yes to belong in the garden

Because despite feels like family to every believer
       who longs to love this world
like a garden where no one's hungry

Because hunger and love are easily mixed up
       when up from some new guy's behind
out falls his evil olive

Because boys will be boys and later men
       who must love despite knowing losers
must eat all the olives

Because briars grow in our garden beside
       belonging and uncultivated running
let them say together we tried

Because what they did not to me so much
       as to another who like me had to
learn this too was our garden

Reflection

I reflect on evil while shaving with a razor
        I bought at Dollar General. Main place

where my father shopped. Deals went
        down inside and out. Still do. Jung said

the reason for evil is that people can't tell
        their true stories. Amazing, I thought—

my father growing a mustache in his last
        year, alone but for neighbors he met at Dollar

General. I once worried a little evil lived
        within my father, but time swapped worry

for heart pills I deposited in a flip-top
        box of days. Below Dollar General's great

canary-backed letters, our town went down.
        Beauty shop tanked, even the barber. Took

five years without my mother before
        a mustache arose silvery above his lips.

Resurrection came my Jungian assessment, hair
        soon our best connection, thin but there.

My father stilled in the chair as I ran clippers
        over his scalp, lifting his chin when it came

to his mustache, trusting his lips to my scissors.
        I snipped on an angle, careful to leave no blood

or evil in our story, only parts he needed telling.

That Monday

Light stretched long on the floor
      another sun awakening
to a scented candle
      aflame in the red jar
atop a picture book, *Mississippi* on
      its spine...

the metal coffee
      table we put together, a cheap
      but practical thing before
the brick-charred air an empty
fireplace leaves, aromatic as another
      image to unleaf, too many
      flowers to identify any
      one among the complication, phlox

maybe, honeysuckle, the sweet showroom

scent where you're supposed to
      pick one among mud-colored
      caskets, that morning's

work, this day's flame, bronze burnished
      to lavender, wax liquified by heat, that
      cologne as you pass by...

Pearl Street Gardenia

In place of a sapling
that under sidewalk tree box
conditions just couldn't

make it, in alabaster
petals and perimeter tints
of urine, the blossoms

persevere in a sweet
odor's sorrow, buds atilt
to people prone to bending

over, to the brief
study of a mitten or banged-up
sippy cup. Things

change like people
once they're no longer
wanted, the street no easy

science. For a dropped
pacifier does not prove every
baby is crying. A ripped

lotto ticket marks no one
a loser. Truth, as the good lover
teaches, begins in glint

or whisper, the touch
of a revealing blossom.
The sidewalk is at peace

with the bother.
Every bus is humbled
once a stop arrives.

The wheeze goes
with a courteous bow before
the door opens.

It is the quaint
visitation of overlooked
effort, the scent

of a gardenia settling
on the same nerve an elderly
clerk in the cafeteria

checkout line tried
to calm when handing over
my change.

The lady never looked
up, attention fixed on my waiting
palm, eyes settling

on creases before
saying as she passed me the cash
I never bothered

to count—
Thank you, Sweetie.

Clarity

Intensive care stays with you.
Patient, nurse, tech, or doctor, here—
why you're here doesn't matter.
Work invariably, this buzzing.
Buzzing stays with you, but try not
to remember you're staying
these days as much as living.
Staying is never easy.
Doubters should ask the nurses.
Alone in bed, or before the bed—
hurt stays with you better
than remembering. You tell yourself
you do the best you can and then
you move on. You tell machines
to do the best they can
until your body does the best
it can also, intensive in
your care, intensive in its
hurt, intensive in its
clarity, this work
of bleach and crafty
bandages, elastic ones
ripped from a roll you
always keep in your pocket.

Six-Step Validation Elegy for Monroe Garment

1. Before sealing the remains, align each hand, one over the other.

Respect positions, broken wings and tarnished inventory:
stainless counters, boys who cut the khaki, Singer machines, steel pressing
tables, bent fathers, birds trapped in the building.

2. Brush her cheeks with rouge, his brow matte powder.

Don't belabor opinions. Just formalize the fluttering:
the cutback and those written up, the one told off, time and a half,
who deserved it, loud mouths like young buzzards, grounded.

3. Tilt the heads so every chin appears determined.

Plan laughs about the trivial:
nights when power failed, meltdowns over nothing, backs caught,
an early closing, doors slammed, outside sparrows flocking.

4. Rather than silk, consider acrylic pillows. They're cheaper.

Prepare the greeters:
practical talk, like beauty shop hullabaloo, the joy
in staying put, in clipped wings and entertaining adultery.

5. Fasten a white rose to his lapel, a pale orchid low below her collar.

Poster-board some pictures:
pleats on invigorating cotton, camo cuts
and creases in strategic places, maybe an album, pages for flitting.

6. Open the lids in every parlor, each face displayed, all music light gospel.

One evocative recording piped in per body:
payday rhythms and production line harmony, trucks backing up at the
loading dock, pinging before birds scurry, shouts as we fly away.

Sediment

they taught us   the Mississippi starts
with raindrops sweeping   loose heartland soil
into wild tumble   before uniting again
within the stream's plunge   a reunion in power
cutting across this   dirty earth as we figured
all power must   cut until we felt some other
testy   forces at work   among
moments   when a river
widened   within us
to reveal a darkness   some bad nature roiling
amidst all the good   we wanted to believe
this world was   more than any dirty river
that's always flowing   with worry
or any feeling   that might leave our fears shushing
between   the state we grew up in
and all those others   we pictured better
power much as within us   power
personalizes a grit   that settles only once
doubt's slithering wake   turns and moonlight
falls on   this soiled surface
this beautiful power   they taught us
to feel as if feeling   itself
might bring us   closer to its maker

Ole Dog

our ole dog hides in a crawl space beneath
the house   safe
in the crawl space, suffering and thankful
maybe for a safe suffering
space   we'll never know
though it's got to hear us
                             stepping on the wooden
floor above, suffering maybe best
in a crawl space if you have to
come home to   suffering
          as an ole dog must, which our
          sounds above probably indicate we
sometimes must also, here above the crawl
space where our ole dog likely   never
considers how we might suffer
                             above, how we might want
nothing more than to curl up
                             beneath the racket and rest
                             our bones as you might
                             want to rest your bones if
you were an ole dog feeling up the earth
                             you dug out in a crawl
                             space, here under voices
                             saying things
                             you feel safer below, you
alone with the earth
                             in filling up the hole

Jack

My father kept big
Jack out back at the barn, the ass
alone with unimaginable

wanting, braying
in gory, two-honk eruptions.
Agony transcended our living

room walls—Jack
pinned in a stall to save the herd—
my father explained, recliner

back down, both
feet up. In the corner, TV's shapely
Vanna turned for

a vowel
my mother in her living years
would have guessed: "O…"

My father loved
the game, Vanna strapless before
the wheel. Simple

words, my father
attentive to the revealing game.
For old Jack was bad

to trample his foals, a killing
that made the momma's milk dry up,
her pelvis realign

for Jack's return, his body's
craving so strong—my father implied—
that need so fatal.

His tone was factual,
careful not to condemn such nature nor
condone it. Come

his final months, my father
needed help, Jack ready as ever at feeding
time. Hand-cupping

crushed corn before Jack's
barbaric mouth, my father would tip
the bucket, his soothing just

so for the horny old
bastard, a brazen patience I feared
I couldn't repeat

when the time came.
But, Vanna, I held the bucket until
big Jack was done, and I

patted his brow, that spot
my father would touch with a word I always
guessed was *Good*. Like love

when you can't figure it
out. Or monstrous braying, where it comes
from. How you know.

In the Derelict Place, a Window

You might think someone left the old recliner
            behind for a new purpose, springs shot, footrest
level with head, the chair turned, so from the window
            what you see is less what it was and more
a plump letter *V* in abandoned profile.
            A ruined thing in a derelict place, the window
has reframed the worn-out stuffing, flexed
            the spine to favor the hard starting letter in a word
like *vanity* or *valor*, a grin spray-painted on the wall.
            If only we might trash our failures among outlived
possessions, hurt reclining within desire's backroom
            decay, so indentations tatter like promising
positions that invariably give when we must leave
            our broken parts to get better. Behind
a shattered window, a *V* rests in trashed silhouette—
            one letter leftover from the slow decomposition
of *lover*—the chair back plush in buttoned down.

Heap

Practical as a pipe, my father is a virtual conduit
                                in aluminum
not premade verbatim   more *de novo*
once he kills the engine at the town dump—
          truck door opening
          and him stepping into a tossed out
vision—my father caterwauling
at the luck in
          our glory, the two of us prowling
          the rich stink of heaped-up stuff he wants
more because it's unwanted—my father
yee-hawing   like a hillbilly
      him yelling *Hell Fire!*   while I hear
every restrung version of *happy*

His yodel and twang   pluck
at the soul in an art   based on
leftovers and bum promises
any boy might toss out   with his father

                              Bent wand of power washer
silver shoot of maimed weed-eater—
          there are so many   so many worthless
          pieces heaped between a man and his boy

They say my father's father could be a mean man
                    I knew him as broken—
wadded   burnt   unraveled
                              shiny parts sticking out—
my father reaching for the metal

The Last Supper
(With Men Under Controlled Conditions)

Behold the strength it takes to paint over a wall
of trouble, to fear better than reveal, our moments

too fleshed-out for containing, one guy too much
a Mary, another all argument, our mass muddling

ear-to-mouth above the gossip table, everyone
hoping hunger alone might preempt the telling

kiss, this illusion the artist and his god apparently
left us to illuminate, our truth in trichrome

spectacle, our fish stinking forever in pieces
we love like the unforgettable and unforgivable,

our traditional bread so broken it's perfected
only by a scream, all of us too messed up to allow

anyone to be properly fingered, our mass too
beholding to the wall that even if destroyed will never

have been untouched by our positions, as trusting
as we are in the point of our stories, as fragile as we

must be to believe in matters we pray to undo even
before they're done, this hunger to erase what we have

been and might be again, this nature the master said
we must behold, before man-to-man, we eat.

ICU 101: How to Intubate the Trachea

Align your head with that of the body
on the table, lifting your eyes above
the mouth, assuming this is a controlled
process, narcotic in and last, of course,
a paralytic, so muscles hang limp
as you thumb up the chin, your fingers then
spreading the lips until the blade impales
the base of the epiglottis, which looks
like the spry bill of a pale baseball
cap, that little guard quaintly curled and stiff as
though hardened from the welding sparks that
flew when your father bent close to the torch,
but you can't dwell on what he had to do,
for you must lift the blade, must lift that
customized covering above the body
that's yours to keep going, for the vocal pillars—
two cords parted but still touching upfront—
welcome you into its nature, its breath
yours to control as if your own, no steps
to undo before implanting a tube
between walls of the only process
you were ever really looking for.

Blackberry Winter

To belong, to contribute, to have
been and still be—

        the dark morning
        birds are beyond squawking.

Rain—joyless as a bad
decision—has finally stopped.

        Caladium fronds hang
        spineless over the pot's blue lip.

Deep down, what's not
lifeless is suffering.

        Only ferns rejoice
        in their damp residue.

They tower
like spiders seeking success

        in drier corners, which flies
        and precocious gnats covet

for similar reasons.
If only our years didn't bondage

        our bodies like celestial
        tasers.

Spiders simply follow
their needs, ferns

        their nature. A horsefly
        does what it must.

Even big
death is inconsequential.

Of failure or death,
birds could care less.

They go blameless
as weather.

Work is a warbled throat,
an appointment

we make to keep
the daylight coming.

NOTES

"Prelude" honors the search and rescue efforts of survivors who, in their diligence, share in the awakening stories that resonate with a new meaning for the word "victim." Lizette Alvarez provided the report of the Smithville, Mississippi tornado in the April 29, 2011, edition of *The New York Times*.

"Zeus" reconfigures the Greek myth of Leda and the swan, in which the king of the gods morphed into a swan before sneaking upon the beautiful princess Leda. Once Leda embraced the swan, Zeus broke from his animal body and ravished the princess. The myth supposedly underscores the potential for terror within beauty, our innate desire for beauty a self-creating feature (arguably, a flaw) within the body we otherwise might reign over. Another myth speaks of Zeus transforming into a bull, his goal this time the seduction of a princess named Europa. Europa also fell for the beauty of the powerful bull, who changed back into the king of the gods once he was alone with the princess. The progeny of Europa and Zeus gave birth to western civilization, as well as the idea that the potential for change accompanies every recognition of a feeling. "The Bull" dwells within the risk of transformation by a feeling.

"Abloom" opens with a Patrick Modiano quote from his novel *Sundays in August*, translated from the French by Damion Searls (Yale University Press).

"Just a Man" honors the "First Lady of Country Music" Tammy Wynette, who was born in the hills near Smithville. In 2024, the Tammy Wynette Legacy Park was welcoming visitors at 10130 Highway 178 East in Tremont, Mississippi. "Stand by Your Man" was Miss Wynette's signature hit.

"Vulcan" expands on the symbolism within the world's largest cast iron statue, which has overlooked Birmingham, Alabama since the 1930's.

"Initiation, in Blue and Eagle," references the work of Leonardo da Vinci, who painted *The Last Supper* on the north wall of a Milan refectory between 1495 and 1497. To preserve the mural painting, the environment within the refectory is stringently controlled. "A sophisticated monitoring device ensures that the air composition and the light and humidity levels remain within the established limits" (UNESCO). Other poems in this collection also reference the mural.

"Crystal Bridges" cites the Crystal Bridges Museum of American Art in Bentonville, Arkansas. The Walton Family Foundation fully funded the acquisitions and endowed the museum with more than 800 million dollars.

"*Tityus, in Black Chalk on Antique Paper*" refers to a Renaissance drawing. In Greek mythology, Tityus was a giant birthed from the earth. The giant's attempts to seduce beautiful humans were so incessant, Zeus punished Tityus by casting him into an immortality of frustration and pain. For vultures were always pecking away at Tityus, and the once powerful man was forever trying to push them back from his body. The myth of Tityus is similar to that of Prometheus, whose kindness to humans was punished by the gods—an eagle forever pecking at his flesh. The myths seem to illustrate the strange jealousy of the gods, who hate to recognize a portion of themselves within every human being. Michelangelo may have been thinking of the bit of divinity within man when he composed his "divine drawings" of Tityus as a gift for his pupil (and supposed lover) Tommaso dei Cavalieri.

"The Girl" owes thoughts of time and men to the writings of Henri Bergson and William Shakespeare.

"Initiation, in Because and Olives" expands upon a quote from Faulkner's 1954 essay entitled, "Mississippi."

"Jack" is a male donkey; a mule is the offspring of a horse and a jack.

ACKNOWLEDGMENTS

Red Camaro celebrates the kindness and irrevocable humanity of my teachers, whom I also call friends and family. The list is lengthy, but I especially value the challenge of Gregory Pardlo, who in 2013 dared me to write a poem about the work of medicine ("ICU 101: How to Intubate the Trachea"). The challenge came in a class that I joined following a decade of having read little poetry and intentionally writing none. It was a period of silence that had followed the death of my mother in 2004. Greg effectively plugged me once more behind the wheel of a relentless red Camaro, which the poems followed.

This collection also honors the great assistance of my writing friends, Rachael Sokolowski, Jennifer Shneiderman, and Véronique Béquin. The poems were also crafted with the grand insights of Kaveh Akbar, Kristina Marie Darling and David Rigsbee.

This collection also celebrates the great staff and supporters of the Cornerstone Press, especially Grace Dahl, Kylie Newton, Cora Bender, Kaydee Rennie, and Dr. Ross Tangedal. This collection would not have been possible without the love and support of my husband, Gregory Bolton, and all the other heroes within my Mississippi family.

Thanks also to the staff of the following journals and magazines, who honored the poems with publication.

Breakwater Review: "How to Intubate the Trachea"

Crack the Spine: "You Should See the Moon Tonight"

Delta Poetry Review: "Crystal Bridges," "Just a Man," "Sediment"

Gone Lawn: "The Animal Table 1," "The Animal Table 2"

Gravel: "Blackberry Winter"

Hunger Mountain Review: "Power Take Off"

Image Journal: "Men's Shop"

Liquid Imagination: "Tityus, in Black Chalk on Antique Paper"

Orson's Review: "The Bull," "Pearl Street Gardenia"

Phi Kappa Phi Forum Magazine: "Zeus"

Pine Row Press: "Overdrawn"

Reservoir Road Literary Review: "Abloom"

Sisyphus: "In the Derelict Place, a Window"

South Caroline Review: "Factory"

Streetlight Magazine: "Red Road"

Susurrus—A Literary Arts Magazine of the South: "In France, the Charolais Never Listen," "Ole Dog"

The BookEnds Review: "When Asked What They Wanted to Do, Mavis Never Changes Her Answer"

The New Guard: "Tarzan"

Thimble Literary Magazine: "Life Cycle"

Touchstone Literary Magazine: "Jamboree"

White Wall Review: "Nona"

Zone 3 Literary Journal: "Heap"

DWAINE RIEVES is the author of *When the Eye Forms* (2005) and *Shirtless Men Drink Free* (2019). He was born and raised in Monroe County, Mississippi. Following a career as a research pharmaceutical scientist and critical care physician, he completed an MA in writing from Johns Hopkins University. His poetry has won the Tupelo Press Prize for Poetry and the River Styx International Poetry Prize, and his writing has appeared in *The Washington Post*, *The Baltimore Sun*, *Virginia Quarterly Review*, *The Georgia Review*, and other publications.

Visit his website at www.dwainerieves.com.